MARKS OF ETERNAL LIFE

By
J. Paul Reno
Pastor and Author

Copyrighted © by Pastor Paul Reno
Hagerstown, MD
December, 2016

ISBN 978-0-9968079-7-5

Published by
Blessed Hope Publishers
Hagerstown, Md.

Publishing and Formatting Assisted by
The Old Paths Publications
142 Gold Flume Way
Cleveland, GA 30528
Web address: www.theoldpathspublications.com
Email address: TOP@theoldpathspublications.com

All Scripture quotations in this book are taken from the King James Version of the Bible. **This work contains the full text of 1 John.**

"All scripture is given by inspiration of God, and is profitable for doctrine, for reproof, for correction, for instruction in righteousness.

That the man of God may be perfect, throughly furnished unto all good works."

(II Tim. 3:16, 17)

DEDICATION

Dedicated to Deacon Harold D. Jones, a praying servant. He has proved himself faithful and invaluable in the various seasons of church life.

Chapter 1 of First John

1Jo 1:1 That which was from the beginning, which we have heard, which we have seen with our eyes, which we have looked upon, and our hands have handled, of the Word of life;

2 (For the life was manifested, and we have seen it, and bear witness, and shew unto you that eternal life, which was with the Father, and was manifested unto us;)

3 That which we have seen and heard declare we unto you, that ye also may have fellowship with us: and truly our fellowship is with the Father, and with his Son Jesus Christ.

4 And these things write we unto you, that your joy may be full.

5 This then is the message which we have heard of him, and declare unto you, that God is light, and in him is no darkness at all.

6 If we say that we have fellowship with him, and walk in darkness, we lie, and do not the truth:

7 But if we walk in the light, as he is in the light, we have fellowship one with another, and the blood of Jesus Christ his Son cleanseth us from all sin.

8 If we say that we have no sin, we deceive ourselves, and the truth is not in us.

9 If we confess our sins, he is faithful and just to forgive us our sins, and to cleanse us from all unrighteousness.

10 If we say that we have not sinned, we make him a liar, and his word is not in us.

TABLE OF CONTENTS

INTRODUCTION

I John 1:1-7

"That which was from the beginning, which we have heard, which we have seen with our eyes, which we have looked upon, and our hands have handled, of The Word of life; (For the life was manifested, and we have seen it, and bear witness, and shew unto you that eternal life, which was with the Father, and was manifested unto us:) That which we have seen and heard declare we unto you, that ye also may have fellowship with us: and truly our fellowship is with the Father, and with His Son Jesus Christ. And these things write we unto you, that your joy may be full. This then is the message which we have heard of Him, and declare unto you, that God is light, and in Him is no darkness at all. If we say that we have fellowship with Him and walk in darkness, we lie, and do not the truth. If we walk in the light, as He is in the light, we have fellowship one with another, and the blood of Jesus Christ His Son cleanseth us from all sin."

Marks of Eternal Life

I would like to examine the marks of eternal life. Often we use terms from the Bible but don't have clear definitions or descriptions of them. Others use the same terms and mean something entirely different. We have come to a time and to a generation that uses the terms but doesn't know what they mean.

God gives us, in His Word, some marks whereby we might know if we are saved. I have found the book of I John to be helpful for people sorting out where they really stand with the Lord. I John will encourage and assure those who are saved, and it will often alarm and awaken those who are lost. Just a simple reading and re-reading with examination will do this.

Days of Confusion

We live in a day of confusion. At the turn of the last century R.A. Torrey said he suspected that eighty percent of the people in Bible-believing churches had never been born again. Billy Graham stated many years ago, that if one out of five of his "converts" were, in fact, saved he would be happy. That is a more honest statement than most people will make. J. Vernon McGee said he believed ninety percent of the Sunday morning crowd who were members in Bible-believing churches in America were lost and would die that way.

The statements of these three men are not being pictured when we are told that we are living in days of revival. We have a generation that claims to have eternal life; but, as we look at I John, I think we will come to the conclusion that many don't actually have any marks of eternal life.

Three Purposes of the Book of 1 John

There are **three purposes** given in the book of I John for its having been written. The **first** purpose is in chapter I verse 4:

> *"And these things write we unto you that your joy might be full."*

If I John did nothing more than fill us with joy wouldn't we want to read it? After all, the joy of the Lord is our strength; and this book promises full joy. We may want to read it with this in mind.

A **second** purpose is given in chapter 2, verse 1a:

*"My little children, these things write I unto you,
that ye sin not."*

This book has been written to help us get out of sin and stop sinning. That is reason enough to read the book through again.

Chapter 5 verse 13 says,

*"These things have I written unto you that believe
on the name of the Son of God; that ye may know
that ye have eternal life, and that ye may believe
on the name of the Son of God."*

This book was written that people might have assurance of salvation. We can know we are saved.

We don't have to hope we are saved or wish we were saved; we can <u>know</u> that we are saved. In fact, the key word to the book of I John is "know". This then is the **third** purpose for the book. I John will help you to know if you are saved, but and if you are not saved it may help you to come to the Savior. The verse also says,

"that ye may believe."

Two Themes

There are **two themes** found in the book of I John; and they are in chapter 5 verse 20:

*"And we know that the Son of God is come, and
hath given us an understanding, that we may
know Him that is true, and we are in Him that is
true, even in His Son Jesus Christ. This is the true
God, and eternal life."*

Notice the ending: "This is the true God and eternal life." These are the two great themes.

The Themes In 1 John

The **first** were purposes; what the book will do for you. **Secondly** we have the two themes: who is the eternal God and what is eternal life.

I know we can read Genesis to Revelation and know all about God. Still, isn't it helpful to know that all of these lines of thought about God will surface somewhere in the book of I John? Some may want to go through the book of I John several times and develop a series of points on the marks of the true God as opposed to what people believe about God.

What Is Eternal Life?

Eternal life is <u>not</u> how long we are going to last. Lost people exist as long as saved people, just in a different place. The lost do not have eternal life.

Eternal life is <u>not</u> our destiny or where we are headed. Eternal life is the present possession of every believer, and we're not in glory yet.

Again you may ask, "What is eternal life?" In His high priestly prayer, the Lord Jesus Christ answered that very question:

> *"And this is life eternal, that they might know Thee the only true God, and Jesus Christ, whom Thou has sent." (John 17:3)*

A Knowing Relationship

That is the Biblical definition of eternal life. It has to do with being in a knowing relationship with God the Father and God the Son. It is eternal by nature because it is God's life.

Eternal means having no beginning and no ending. It is different from everlasting which means that of going on forever. We get a life that was around long before we existed. It is eternal life; it is God's life that He gives us. The Bible says,

"For the life was manifested, and we have seen it, and bear witness, and shew unto you that eternal life, which was with the Father, and was manifested unto us:" (I John 1:2).

In other words, it came from Him and was shown to us, we received it, and it can be shown to others.

Eternal life is not invisible, unexplainable or unrecognizable. It is something to show and manifest that others might see. We should demonstrate eternal life to a lost and dying world around us. This is not just some religious term we picked up because we said a prayer, made a decision, or went through some kind of religious process. We ought to be able to demonstrate eternal life.

I John 2:25-26 states,

"And this is the promise that He hath promised us, even eternal life. These things have I written unto you concerning them that seduce you."

You Can Know

Why is it so important to make an issue over eternal life? It is important because people will seduce us into thinking we have it when we don't. They will try to draw us away from what is right. We must know what is real and genuine.

"And this is the record, that God hath given to us eternal life, and this life is in His Son" (I John 5:11).

"These things have I written unto you that believe on the name of the Son of God: that ye may know that ye have eternal life, and that you may believe on the name of the Son of God" (I John 5:13).

God wants us to know that we have eternal life. Throughout I John, beginning with chapter 1 and to the end of chapter 5, it comes up again and again. The remainder of this book will focus on the twelve marks of eternal life.

CHAPTER 1

MARK # 1:
FELLOWSHIP WITH GOD THE FATHER AND JESUS CHRIST

Let us begin with the first mark of eternal life.

"That which we have seen and heard declare we unto you, that ye also may have fellowship with us: and truly our fellowship is with the Father and with His Son Jesus Christ" (I John 1:3).

The **first mark** of eternal life is that we have fellowship with both God the Father and God the Son. Lost people can't have that. Saved people not only <u>can</u> but <u>do</u> have that. This fellowship is real. It is an intimate communion, - as real and as trustworthy as anything you might experience in the human realm. We can never be sure about other people, but God we can trust. We can open our hearts to Him. We can talk with Him and listen to Him. We will come to enjoy His presence. The fellowship is as real as that of a husband and wife (Eph. 5). It is as real as that of a father and his children as taught in the pattern prayer,

"Our Father which art in heaven . . . ."

We are to have and enjoy that kind of fellowship. It is not the fellowship of a dysfunctional family, but of a fully functional family. It is intimate fellowship.

Will this fellowship always be there? There are times that it may be broken; and that will grieve our hearts. We will want to make things right. A real sense of fellowship and communion with Deity is a mark of eternal life. It is something that sets us apart from those who are still dead in their trespasses and sins.

It is possible to be religious and fundamental and lost. A number of years ago I was preaching in a Bible conference. On the final night, I was called over to visit with a couple who had become increasingly troubled. The husband had been through Bible school, held to the fundamental truths of the Scriptures and had been a pastor. He said, "We have a number of questions about what you have been preaching this week. You speak about knowing Jesus like you know your wife. How can that be?"

I explained, "When I was saved, I entered into a relationship with Jesus like a bride enters into with her groom." He readily agreed that such was Biblical. I continued, "The Bible not only teaches that, but it is exactly what happens." I went on to question as to whether he was indeed married. His reply was forceful. "Yes!" I couldn't convince him that his marriage was a figment of his imagination and only in his mind.

I avowed that, just as surely, he would know when he got saved. Salvation is real in the soul. This poor man didn't know anything of fellowshipping with God. He had only learned doctrine and preached doctrine.

We have a generation that responds very well to fellowshipping with one another, but they don't grasp that real fellowship is not so much with people but with the God behind the people. Fellowship with God is a mark of eternal life. Do we have this mark?

I John 1:6 reads,

> "If we say that we have fellowship with Him, and
> walk in darkness, we lie and do not the truth."

He is saying that if we walk in darkness and claim to have fellowship with God we are lying. We are not doing truth.

Walking in the light is not optional. Fellowship is related to our earthly walk. We are to walk in the light.

I John 1:7

I John 1:7 says,

> *"If we walk in the light as He is in the light, we have fellowship one with another and the blood of Jesus Christ His Son cleanseth us from all sin."*

Today it is common for people who have never known what it is to walk in the light or to have fellowship with God to claim the merits of the blood of Christ. We have no right to the blood of Jesus unless we are willing to be saved out of darkness, and are willing to be brought into the kingdom of light, and are ready to fellowship with both the Father and the Son. It is only then that the blood does anything in a practical way for our sin. The idea that we can live as we please, confess our sin and be forgiven, and continue to live like we please is directly opposed to the teaching of the Bible and is contrary to the marks of eternal life. That sounds strong, but God is just warming to the subject of what eternal life really is.

What is the nature of this fellowship that marks eternal life? I John 4:19 states,

> *"We love Him, because He first loved us."*

How did He love us? He loved us with a sacrificial love. We should respond with our sacrificial love. Those who don't have a sacrificial love for God raise a question as to whether they have ever known the love of God in their souls. Do they, in truth, know anything about eternal life?

We don't have fellowship with our enemies, but with those we love. The more we love an individual, the deeper the fellowship runs. Hopefully it is met with a deep, responding love.

I John 5:2

In I John 5:2 we read,

"By this we know that we love the children of God and keep His commandments."

Our love for God will be shown in our obedience. Not only will we respond with a sacrificial love, but we will also respond with an obedient love. Fellowship between a husband and wife breaks down when they quit sacrificing for each other, and they won't be obedient to their marriage vows.

1 John 2:6

Look at chapter 2 verse 6:

"He that saith he abideth in Him ought himself also so to walk, even as He walked."

The fellowship is going to affect our lives so that we will follow the life of the Lord Jesus Christ. He will be our pattern – not some athlete, businessman, politician, educator or military hero. Jesus becomes the pattern for our lives and we walk accordingly. That is the clear evidence of fellowship. It is easy to tell with whom people have been fellowshipping. Watch how they live.

"Herein is our love made perfect, that we may have boldness in the day of judgment: because as He is, so are we in this world" (I John 4:17).

As Jesus is right now, so are we in this world. How can that be? It is one thing to be like Him when we actually see Him, but it is another to be like Him in this world before we see Him.

Fellowshipping with Him and being in love with Him are bound to affect us. We are becoming and demonstrating what He is. This eternal life is not just a term. It can be seen, felt, and demonstrated; and it ought to be enjoyed. Life eternal is knowing Him the only true God, and knowing Jesus Christ whom God the Father sent. It is a knowing relationship and fellowship.

Chapter 2 of 1 John

1Jo 2:1 My little children, these things write I unto you, that ye sin not. And if any man sin, we have an advocate with the Father, Jesus Christ the righteous:
2 And he is the propitiation for our sins: and not for ours only, but also for the sins of the whole world.
3 And hereby we do know that we know him, if we keep his commandments.
4 He that saith, I know him, and keepeth not his commandments, is a liar, and the truth is not in him.
5 But whoso keepeth his word, in him verily is the love of God perfected: hereby know we that we are in him.
6 He that saith he abideth in him ought himself also so to walk, even as he walked.
7 Brethren, I write no new commandment unto you, but an old commandment which ye had from the beginning. The old commandment is the word which ye have heard from the beginning.
8 Again, a new commandment I write unto you, which thing is true in him and in you: because the darkness is past, and the true light now shineth.
9 He that saith he is in the light, and hateth his brother, is in darkness even until now.
10 He that loveth his brother abideth in the light, and there is none occasion of stumbling in him.
11 But he that hateth his brother is in darkness, and walketh in darkness, and knoweth not whither he goeth, because that darkness hath blinded his eyes.
Continued on next page:

12 *I write unto you, little children, because your sins are forgiven you for his name's sake.*

13 *I write unto you, fathers, because ye have known him that is from the beginning. I write unto you, young men, because ye have overcome the wicked one. I write unto you, little children, because ye have known the Father.*

14 *I have written unto you, fathers, because ye have known him that is from the beginning. I have written unto you, young men, because ye are strong, and the word of God abideth in you, and ye have overcome the wicked one.*

15 *Love not the world, neither the things that are in the world. If any man love the world, the love of the Father is not in him.*

16 *For all that is in the world, the lust of the flesh, and the lust of the eyes, and the pride of life, is not of the Father, but is of the world.*

17 *And the world passeth away, and the lust thereof: but he that doeth the will of God abideth for ever.*

18 *Little children, it is the last time: and as ye have heard that antichrist shall come, even now are there many antichrists; whereby we know that it is the last time.*

19 *They went out from us, but they were not of us; for if they had been of us, they would no doubt have continued with us: but they went out, that they might be made manifest that they were not all of us.*

20 *But ye have an unction from the Holy One, and ye know all things.*

21 *I have not written unto you because ye know not the truth, but because ye know it, and that no lie is of the truth.*

22 *Who is a liar but he that denieth that Jesus is the Christ? He is antichrist, that denieth the Father and the Son.*

23 *Whosoever denieth the Son, the same hath not the Father: (but) he that acknowledgeth the Son hath the Father also.* **Continued on the next page:**

24 Let that therefore abide in you, which ye have heard from the beginning. If that which ye have heard from the beginning shall remain in you, ye also shall continue in the Son, and in the Father.

25 And this is the promise that he hath promised us, *even* eternal life.

26 These *things* have I written unto you concerning them that seduce you.

27 But the anointing which ye have received of him abideth in you, and ye need not that any man teach you: but as the same anointing teacheth you of all things, and is truth, and is no lie, and even as it hath taught you, ye shall abide in him.

28 And now, little children, abide in him; that, when he shall appear, we may have confidence, and not be ashamed before him at his coming.

29 If ye know that he is righteous, ye know that every one that doeth righteousness is born of him.

CHAPTER 2

MARK # 2
RECOGNIZE YOU ARE A SINNER

The second mark of eternal life is given in I John, chapter 1, verses 8-10:

> "*If we say that we have no sin, we deceive ourselves, and the truth is not in us. If we confess our sins, He is faithful and just to forgive us our sins, and to cleanse us from all unrighteousness. If we say that we have not sinned, we make Him a liar, and His word is not in us.*"

Again, this is strong language, but God is using it because it is true. The second mark of eternal life is that we recognize that we are sinners.

There are those who think they live above sin. We really cannot fool anyone else, and we certainly cannot fool God. The only we you may fool is ourself. Everyone else will realize we are sinners.

Early in my ministry I was given a contact to visit a man named Tom. He lived a few miles down the road in the next school district. Upon my arrival, Tom claimed to be saved, and sinless since he was a boy. He believed it! He was deceiving himself. I asked if I could read some Scripture. I slowed down when I came to verse 8 in the first chapter of I John:

> "*If we say that we have no sin, we deceive ourselves, and the truth is not in us.*"

Tom didn't know what to do with this verse because he wanted to think he had no sin. However, God says that those who say they have no sin do <u>not</u> have the truth in them.

In John 14, Jesus said to His disciples, "*I am the way, the truth . . . .*" Perhaps one of the clearest definitions of truth is the Lord Jesus Christ. Jesus is the truth! If we substitute the Lord Jesus Christ for the word "truth" in verse 8 the verse says that Jesus Christ is not in us. That is a fatal flaw.

Go to John 17 verse 17, where Jesus is praying,

> "*Sanctify them through Thy truth; Thy Word is truth.*"

When truth is not in us, the Word, or the Scripture, is not in us. A little later in I John we will find that it says the Spirit is truth. A person who vows that they have no sin in essence says there is no Jesus, no Scripture and no Holy Spirit within.

When Jesus is inside us, He is so pure and holy, we have to face that we have sin. If the Word of God is also in us it will expose that sin; and if the Holy Spirit is within, He will convict us of that sin. To go on believing that you have no sin is to say, "I don't have anyone or anything within to show me what I really am. I don't have eternal life. I am blind, and I am dead in my trespasses and sins."

1 John 1:10

In I John 1:10 we read,

> "*If we say that we have not sinned, we make Him a liar, and His Word is not in us.*"

A number of years ago a lady in our church brought a friend to our home to talk with us. She didn't seem to have much assurance of her salvation and wanted some help in that area. It is the Holy Spirit's job to give assurance; and I figured if she was not getting it through Him, there must be a reason.

I began to ask questions; but, knowing the book of I John, I didn't need to ask many before I knew she was lost. I asked her to tell me about her salvation. She told me where she was, when it was and what she did. I then asked her from what she was saved . She responded that she was saved from hell. Finally, after a few more questions, she decided she must have been saved from sin. When I asked pointedly from what sins she was saved, she responded, "You know. Sin. We're all sinners." She thought of sin merely in a generic sense, but never had she felt guilt from having committed any certain sins.

I am afraid there are too many church members walking in the same shoes she walked in. Her husband or children could have told her what her sins were. In that the Bible says Christ Jesus came into the world specifically to save sinners, she was in no position to get saved! He didn't come for the righteous.

Have you, dear reader, ever seen yourself as one who has violated the laws of God? Have you seen yourself as a sinner who is guilty before a holy God? If you have never seen this, you do not have eternal life. God's gift of eternal life will make sin stick out like a fly on a white wall. However, if your soul is still in darkness, sin is like a fly on a black wall. You will never notice the sin.

> *"My little children, these things write I unto you,*
> *that ye sin not . . . ."*

These things are not written to encourage us in our sin or to give us sympathy, refuge or comfort. This is written to get us out of our sin.

> *"And if any man sin, we have an advocate with*
> *the Father, Jesus Christ the righteous: And He is*
> *the propitiation for our sins: and not for ours*
> *only, but also for the sins of the whole world" (I*
> *John 2:1-2).*

We are not to glory in our sin. We are to hate our sin, strive to stay out of sin, and realize that it costs Jesus every time we get into sin. The second mark of eternal life is that we realize we are a sinner.

CHAPTER 3

MARK #3
KEEP GOD'S COMMANDMENTS

I John 2:3 states,

> *"And hereby we do know that we know Him, if we keep His commandments."*

The third mark of eternal life is that we keep His commandments. We don't casually break or ignore them. Keeping His commandments is the evidence of knowing Jesus, the evidence of eternal life. How do we know if we know Jesus? We will know if we keep His commandments. Anyone can say they know Jesus, but that does not mean they truly know Him. Eternal life is evidenced when we keep His commandments.

Do we keep them perfectly? Our heart says that we want to. Remember, the second mark is that we recognize we are sinners. We will be confessing, repenting, and getting cleansing when we sin. However, we will strive to keep His commandments because we know Him and we love Him. That will be the true pattern of our lives.

God develops this further in verse 4,

> *"He that saith, I know Him and keepeth not His commandments, is a liar, and the truth is not in Him."*

With each of these three marks, God affirms that we must have the mark. If we claim to have the mark and our lives don't line up, we are liars. Lost professors are liars. They bear false witness. They also use the name of the Lord God in vain by claiming it when they have no right. They are in trouble with two of the Ten Commandments.

"But whoso keepeth His word, in him verily is the love of God perfected: hereby know we that we are in Him" (I John 2:5).

Some say, "But I know I am in Christ." How can we know that? Biblically we know it because we are fellowshipping with Him. We recognize we are sinners, but by the grace of God and with the help of God, we are going to live according to the commands of God. We are obedient to what Jesus said to do.

"He that saith he abideth in Him ought himself also so to walk, even as He walked" (I John 2:6).

I believe it was Charles Spurgeon who said that if a man knew the will of God and did not intend to perform it, it was his responsibility to inform such a man that he was unregenerate. That sounds strong, but that is really just repeating what I John 2 teaches. In fact, it may not be quite as strong as the Scripture because Mr. Spurgeon was not calling such a man a liar; God did.

Presently, we have a generation that feels the will of God is optional. The commands of God don't even need to be studied. Even less, do they need to be lived out. This same generation continues to think they are heaven bound.

Recently a man spoke to me after I had preached. For years he had thought he was saved but wasn't. Just a few years ago he was genuinely born again. He said, "Earlier, if you had asked me, I would have told you I was saved. You couldn't have talked me out of it. It wasn't until God showed me, that I realized I was truly lost. I had planned to live as I wanted. Now I see how wrong I was."

There are many such who believe they are going to heaven and the way they live doesn't make any difference. How we live will let us know whether we might be going to heaven. Understand, we don't get there by works; but we are not likely to get there without any! A faith that doesn't produce works is a dead faith. Eternal life can readily be seen in the life of the believer.

> *"And the world passeth away, and the lust thereof: but he that doeth the will of God abideth forever"* (I John 2:17).

Abiding forever is linked to obedience by God Himself. "And he that keepeth His commandments dwelleth in Him and He in him. And hereby we know that He abideth in us, by the Spirit which He hath given us" (I John 3:24). How do we know if we are in Jesus? The obedient are in Christ, and Christ is in the obedient. These are the ones who have eternal life and will live forever.

I John 5:2-3

I John 5:2-3 says,

> *"By this we know that we love the children of God, when we love God, and keep His commandments. For this is the love of God, that we keep His commandments: and His command- ments are not grievous."*

Some folks are willing to keep His commandments if that is necessary, and they struggle and strain to do so. However, when God saves us He gives us a new nature and makes us a new creature in Christ Jesus. *"Old things are passed away: behold all things are become new."* (II Cor. 5:17b).

He puts His life in us and His life is to be shown to others. It is then that one can say, "His commandments that looked so hard are not so bad after all. I actually delight to do His will." Not delighting in keeping His commandments reveals those who are trying to fake a godly life.

God's own respond to His commands saying, "Well, that is what God said. Hallelujah! What else did He say? I find no grief in keeping His commandments." I have been saved since 1950, and I can honestly say that I have not found any of His commands grievous to me. The closest I came to that grief was when He called me into the ministry. Yet, if that was what He wanted, that settled it. Why was it so simple? I have eternal life. His eternal life will help us to respond, "Not my will but Thy will be done."

Many today are not interested in fellowshipping with God, have not faced the sin issue, and don't want to obey the commands of God. Yet, they insist that they have eternal life. In reality, they are missing the first three marks shown in the book of I John.

A number of years ago, God led me to pastor a church that wanted many activities for their youth. I planned the first street meeting they had ever experienced. We set up in front of some stores in a shopping center on a Saturday night and started the open-air meeting. Various ones had been given responsibilities such as reading Scripture, singing, passing out tracts, or testifying. How well I remember the testimony of one of our young men: "When I got saved, nothing much happened." In a matter of several years, this same young man found he had never been saved.

As a youngster I learned a chorus,
"Something happened when He saved me,
Happened in my heart, happened in my heart,
Something happened when He saved me,
Something happened in my heart."

Certainly, when a person gets saved he moves from darkness to light. He moves out of the kingdom of the devil and into the kingdom of the Lord Jesus Christ. He is no longer headed for hell. He is now heaven bound with a new nature, for old things are passed away and all things have become new. He is a new creature in Christ Jesus. Enormous, radical changes occur.

I do want to reaffirm that each of these marks may not be 100% clearly manifest in our soul. We still have a flesh nature; but if we are really saved, these marks will show up from time to time in varying degrees of strength. There will be holy desires. We won't have to struggle to have these marks; they are normal and natural marks of eternal life.

Chapter 3 of 1 John

1Jo 3:1 Behold, what manner of love the Father hath bestowed upon us, that we should be called the sons of God: therefore the world knoweth us not, because it knew him not.

2 Beloved, now are we the sons of God, and it doth not yet appear what we shall be: but we know that, when he shall appear, we shall be like him; for we shall see him as he is.

3 And every man that hath this hope in him purifieth himself, even as he is pure.

4 Whosoever committeth sin transgresseth also the law: for sin is the transgression of the law.

5 And ye know that he was manifested to take away our sins; and in him is no sin.

6 Whosoever abideth in him sinneth not: whosoever sinneth hath not seen him, neither known him.

7 Little children, let no man deceive you: he that doeth righteousness is righteous, even as he is righteous.

8 He that committeth sin is of the devil; for the devil sinneth from the beginning. For this purpose the Son of God was manifested, that he might destroy the works of the devil.

9 Whosoever is born of God doth not commit sin; for his seed remaineth in him: and he cannot sin, because he is born of God.

10 In this the children of God are manifest, and the children of the devil: whosoever doeth not righteousness is not of God, neither he that loveth not his brother.

11 For this is the message that ye heard from the beginning, that we should love one another.

12 Not as Cain, who was of that wicked one, and slew his brother. And wherefore slew he him? Because his own works were evil, and his brother's righteous.

continued on the next page:

13 Marvel not, my brethren, if the world hate you.

14 We know that we have passed from death unto life, because we love the brethren. He that loveth not his brother abideth in death.

15 Whosoever hateth his brother is a murderer: and ye know that no murderer hath eternal life abiding in him.

16 Hereby perceive we the love of God, because he laid down his life for us: and we ought to lay down our lives for the brethren.

17 But whoso hath this world's good, and seeth his brother have need, and shutteth up his bowels of compassion from him, how dwelleth the love of God in him?

18 My little children, let us not love in word, neither in tongue; but in deed and in truth.

19 And hereby we know that we are of the truth, and shall assure our hearts before him.

20 For if our heart condemn us, God is greater than our heart, and knoweth all things.

21 Beloved, if our heart condemn us not, then have we confidence toward God.

22 And whatsoever we ask, we receive of him, because we keep his commandments, and do those things that are pleasing in his sight.

23 And this is his commandment, That we should believe on the name of his Son Jesus Christ, and love one another, as he gave us commandment.

24 And he that keepeth his commandments dwelleth in him, and he in him. And hereby we know that he abideth in us, by the Spirit which he hath given us.

CHAPTER 4

MARK #4
LIVE RIGHTEOUSLY

Moving to the fourth mark, notice I John 2:29:

> *"If ye know that He is righteous, ye know that every one that doeth righteousness is born of Him."*

The fourth mark shows up in a righteous life—not just imputed righteousness, and not just positional righteousness, but righteous living. This will quickly dispose of those who say, "I am saved and can live like I want."

The mark is this. We know that the ones who DO righteousness, are the ones who are born of God. Those who don't do righteousness, obviously do not have eternal life because eternal life produces a life of active righteousness. This is not passive or potential righteousness. Let me call your attention to the "eth" in doeth. It is the old English way of letting us know this verb is progressive. They do righteously, they keep on doing righteously and they will continue doing righteously. It is not a case that once, some years ago, they did something righteous. "Doeth" means it is ongoing and active.

When God saved us, He saved us to a life of doing, doing, and doing righteously. This is something He put in our heart and empowered us to be able to do. This is a desire and will become a practice. We may not be 100% on target, but we will be grieved when we fail.

In the book of Philippians the Apostle Paul wrote,

> *". . . work out your own salvation with fear and trembling. For it is God which worketh in you*

both to will and to do of His good pleasure" (Phil. 2:12,13).

God's working within us at the time of our salvation will show up as an outworking of righteous deeds. He is the one who works in us to will and to do of His good pleasure. He will have us will to do righteous deeds, and He will have us do them. If we know anything about the righteousness of Jesus, we know that those who have been born again are going to evidence a life similar to that of the Lord Jesus Christ. I expect my children to behave somewhat like I do. I should see some family traits. In the same way, when we are born into the family of God, we ought to manifest "family" traits. People who live like the devil and act like him are showing in which family they really belong. We know that Jesus is righteous. Thus, we automatically know that everyone that is born of Him will do righteousness. A holy life will be produced, and progress will be made in this holiness.

> *"Beloved, now are we the sons of God, and it doth not yet appear what we shall be: but we know that, when He shall appear, we shall be like Him for we shall see Him as He is. And every man that hath this hope in him purifieth himself, even as He is pure"* (I John 3:2-3).

We have a positional purity because Jesus is pure; and we are in Him, and He is in us. But there is also a practical purity. We are doing that which is righteous. We are behaving with the nature and actions of the Lord Jesus Christ.

The hope of the rapture—just knowing that He may be back at any moment makes for pure living. Many folks talk about Jesus' return but show little or no desire to live holy lives. They apparently have no fear that they may stand before Him before the second hand on the clock makes another complete revolution. They seem not to fear being caught at what they are doing. Eternal life makes a difference. It is not worth having if it doesn't.

> *"Little children, let no man deceive you: he that doeth righteousness is righteous, even as He is righteous" (I John 3:7).*

The clear evidence of our positional and imputed righteousness in the Lord Jesus Christ is that we live and do righteously. To claim that we have positional righteousness without the practice is empty talk.

I was ministering in the little island country of Dominica many years ago when we encountered a beggar who caught me by surprise. He didn't beg in the normal fashion of telling how poor and needy he was. Rather, as he came toward us, he announced that he was king of the universe and wanted to shake our hands. My friend, being a little sharper and more experienced at these opportunities than I, said, "Quick, Paul! Get your camera out. I want a picture of me shaking the hand of the king of the universe," The beggar, smiling broadly, seemed honored and turned to pose. As we turned to cross the street, the fellow started crying, "Give me a dollar! Give me a dollar!" My friend countered, "A dollar?! If you are king of the universe you surely don't need a dollar!"

There are many people who say they are righteous, but they can't begin to live righteously. They are making a claim, but there is nothing in their life that backs it up. They claim to be kings and priests while acting like beggars! They further claim that they have been saved and enjoy positional righteousness. All the while, they are defeated by sin. Such folks are unable to do right as hard as they try.

This is a bold contradiction of Scripture. We know that he that doeth righteousness is righteous. Don't be deceived on this. The righteousness of our Lord will enable us to live as He commands. He didn't just settle a debt written on a mere slip of paper in Heaven. No! He made you and me positionally righteous so we could live righteously now. We were incapable of living righteously before we were converted.

"In this the children of God are manifest, and the children of the devil: whosoever doeth not righteousness is not of God, neither he that loveth not his brother," (I John 3:10).

Now those who do righteousness do so because they are righteous and have been born of God. Those who don't do righteousness are of the devil and have never been born of God. In places where persecution is common, churches often watch the lives of professing converts. They want to find out if these folks are, in fact, new creatures before they baptize them. They don't want to be bringing lost people into the church membership, and thereby weakening the strength of the church. They firmly believe that when someone gets truly saved, something will happen in their heart. God will make a difference, and that difference will mean they will live righteously.

I have heard it told that under communism behind the iron curtain, church leaders would visit in the neighborhood where a newly professing believer lived. They would ask if anything had changed in the person's life. Perhaps they would go further and question folks at the person's workplace. If neighbors and co-workers had noticed no changes, the person in question might need to wait another six months for baptism and church membership.

Back in the 1950's, my dad was preaching in Michigan. At the end of the service a man came to speak with him and said, "You know, I have been working in the auto plant for thirty years; and so far, no one has been able to discover that I am a Christian." Dad, not one to raise his voice, quietly commented,

"Perhaps God has not discovered it either." If a person cannot do righteously, it is because he has not been saved.

> "Herein is our love made perfect, that we may
> have boldness in the day of judgment: because as
> He is, so are we in this world" (I John 4:17).

He is righteous, so we will be righteous as well. In a sense, when a person is saved and receives eternal life, he becomes almost an extension of Deity. Jesus said,

> "The works that I do shall he do also; and greater
> works than these shall he do, because I go to my
> Father" (John 14:12b)

Over time we have weakened the definition of salvation until lost people can comfortably satisfy it. As He is-- and He is God-- so are we. People ought to see something in our lives that would point them to God.

Many years ago a missionary to China went into a province where, as far as he knew, there had been no Gospel witness. He approached a village and began preaching about the Lord Jesus Christ. One man quickly raised his hand to say that they knew this man and that he had been there. Thinking he had not been clear enough, the missionary backed up and preached some basic truths once more. Again, he was interrupted. The missionary responded, "No, no. He hasn't been here Himself because He died, rose again, and went back to Heaven a long time ago." Finally a villager ran off and presently came back with a tract. He said, "See. Here is proof. He has been here and left this for us." The missionary carefully looked at the tract and began to weep. This tract was one that one of the godliest missionaries on the field used often. That missionary had, indeed, been there, and his life had shown righteousness so clearly that the people became confused. When they heard about Jesus, they immediately thought of this missionary.

As He is, so are we in this world. Has anyone ever confused us, even for a moment, with the Lord Jesus Christ? There should be something about us that causes onlookers to think of Jesus. I know we are not God. However, He is in us; and we are in Him and empowered by Him.

Edgar Guest wrote the following poem that illustrates this principle:

> I'd rather see a sermon
> than hear one any day;
> I'd rather one should walk
> with me
> than merely tell the way.
> The eye's a better pupil
> and more willing than the
> ear,
> Fine counsel is confusing,
> but example's always clear;
> And the best of all preachers
> are the men who live their
> creeds,
> For to see good put in action
> is what everybody needs.
> I soon can learn to do it
> if you'll let me see it done;
> I can watch your hands in
> action,
> but your tongue too fast
> may run.
> And the lectures you deliver
> may be very wise and true,
> But I'd rather get my lesson

by observing what you do;
For I might misunderstand you
and the high advice you
give,
But there's no misunderstand-
ing
how you act and how you
live.

We are walking sermons. We are evidence of the God we serve and the Christ we love.

Chapter 4 of 1 John

1Jo 4:1 Beloved, believe not every spirit, but try the spirits whether they are of God: because many false prophets are gone out into the world.

2 Hereby know ye the Spirit of God: Every spirit that confesseth that Jesus Christ is come in the flesh is of God:

3 And every spirit that confesseth not that Jesus Christ is come in the flesh is not of God: and this is that spirit of antichrist, whereof ye have heard that it should come; and even now already is it in the world.

4 Ye are of God, little children, and have overcome them: because greater is he that is in you, than he that is in the world.

5 They are of the world: therefore speak they of the world, and the world heareth them.

6 We are of God: he that knoweth God heareth us; he that is not of God heareth not us. Hereby know we the spirit of truth, and the spirit of error.

7 Beloved, let us love one another: for love is of God; and every one that loveth is born of God, and knoweth God.

Continued on the next page:

8 He that loveth not knoweth not God; for God is love.

9 In this was manifested the love of God toward us, because that God sent his only begotten Son into the world, that we might live through him.

10 Herein is love, not that we loved God, but that he loved us, and sent his Son to be the propitiation for our sins.

11 Beloved, if God so loved us, we ought also to love one another.

12 No man hath seen God at any time. If we love one another, God dwelleth in us, and his love is perfected in us.

13 Hereby know we that we dwell in him, and he in us, because he hath given us of his Spirit.

14 And we have seen and do testify that the Father sent the Son to be the Saviour of the world.

15 Whosoever shall confess that Jesus is the Son of God, God dwelleth in him, and he in God.

16 And we have known and believed the love that God hath to us. God is love; and he that dwelleth in love dwelleth in God, and God in him.

17 Herein is our love made perfect, that we may have boldness in the day of judgment: because as he is, so are we in this world.

18 There is no fear in love; but perfect love casteth out fear: because fear hath torment. He that feareth is not made perfect in love.

19 We love him, because he first loved us.

20 If a man say, I love God, and hateth his brother, he is a liar: for he that loveth not his brother whom he hath seen, how can he love God whom he hath not seen?

21 And this commandment have we from him, That he who loveth God love his brother also.

CHAPTER 5

MARK #5
LOVE THE BRETHREN

I John 3:4 says,

> *"We know that we have passed from death unto life, because we love the brethren. He that loveth not his brother abideth in death."*

We don't love brothers and sisters in the Lord because they are lovable. We don't love them because they love us and are sweet and kind, and never say anything negative about us. We love them because we have eternal life within us. God put His love within us for some who are very different from us. That love is an evidence of eternal life. Anyone can love someone who is nice to him, but God puts a love in the believer for someone who may not be nice to him. That is not natural; it is supernatural. It is called eternal life. If you don't love your brother you are not saved.

> *"Whosoever hateth his brother is a murderer: and ye know that no murderer hath eternal life abiding in him"* (I John 3:15).

The fifth mark is that we love other Christians. It lets us know whether we are in life or in death. Verse 16 goes on to say,

> *"Hereby perceive we the love of God, because He laid down His life for us: and we ought to lay down our lives for the brethren."*

God will put such a love in our hearts that we will be willing to risk our lives. If necessary, we will give our lives to help a brother or sister. We will give up sleep to pour our hearts out in prayer.

We will sacrifice our own finances to help a brother or sister and to get the Gospel out. We will push ourselves and pay the price, whatever it is.

I John 3:17 continues,

> "But whoso hath this world's good, and seeth his brother have need, and shutteth up his bowels of compassion from him, how dwelleth the love of God in him?"

It ought to break our hearts to see our brother or sister in need. We ought to do something about that need if we have the ability to do so.

The churches in Macedonia were in great poverty. However, when they heard of the famine that was affecting the saints in Jerusalem, they took up an offering to send to meet the needs of those saints. They had love in their hearts for their brothers and sisters, though they had never met them. They heard of their need and wanted to do something for them. If we really love our brothers and sisters, it will be manifest in a practical way.

Verses 18 and 19 add,

> "My little children, let us not love in word, neither in tongue, but in deed and in truth. And hereby we know that we are of the truth, and shall assure our hearts before him."

We don't just talk so much about how much we love others; we show how much we love them. Some pastors have congregations that readily say how much they love but never bother to try to meet specific needs. We cannot feed a family on words. Deeds are necessary. It is one thing to say, "The Lord bless you." It is quite another matter to be the avenue of blessing that the Lord uses.

Who has ever had more than we Christians here in the United States; but, how much greed and covetousness are we covering up? I must point out that the manifestation of this mark is not something that is worked up. Rather, it is a natural outflow. That is why it assures our hearts. When we hear of a need our heart is touched. We are delighted to realize that our response is different from our lost days. Stinginess in giving is usually evidence of a lost soul.

> *"Though He was rich yet for your sakes He became poor, that ye through His poverty might be rich" (II Cor. 8:9b).*

We ought to be evidencing the same thing in our lives, — seeing how much we can pour out of ourselves and our wealth for the glory and Gospel of God.

> *"This is His commandment, that we should believe on the name of His Son Jesus Christ, and love one another, as He gave us commandment" (I John 3:23).*

This is not optional; it is a command. Chapter 2, verses 9 and 10 say,

> *"He that saith he is in the light and hateth his brother, is in darkness even until now. He that loveth his brother abideth in the light, and there is none occasion of stumbling in him."*

If we truly love our brother, we will do all we can to keep him from stumbling. When visiting in a church service in Egypt, I was careful not to cross my legs because that would be offensive. Those believers feel that sitting with crossed legs is too casual and has no place in worshipping God. That does not mean this is something I enforce upon myself all the time, but I in no way wanted to be the cause of stumbling in those dear Egyptian brothers.

If I were preaching to the Amish I would probably not wear a neck tie as such could be offensive to them. Sadly, this present generation so often wants their rights, and cares little about being a stumbling stone. A conscientious believer who finds he has caused someone to stumble, whether or not he fully understands what the other person feels, should be grieved and endeavor to keep it from happening again. This is Christian love and a part of eternal life.

> *"Beloved, let us love one another: for love is of God; and every one that loveth is born of God, and knoweth God. He that loveth not knoweth not God; for God is love" (I John 4:7,8).*

To show love is simply to show part of the nature He has put within us. If there is no love forthcoming, then we don't know God. This is what the Bible says, and it is a serious matter. Verse 9 continues,

> *"In this was manifested the love of God toward us, because that God sent His only begotten Son into the world, that we might live through Him."*

Verses 11 and 12 say,

> *"Beloved, if God so loved us, we ought also to love one another. No man hath seen God at any time. If we love one another, God dwelleth in us, and His love is perfected in us."*

Very simply put, God loved us, so we ought to love one another.

> *"If a man say, I love God, and hateth his brother, he is a liar: for he that loveth not his brother*

whom he hath seen, how can he love God whom
he hath not seen?" (I John 4:20).

We may feel it is easier to love God because He is perfect; and our brother is not. But remember, we have not seen God. In fact, the only view of God we are going to get is in our brother and sister. We ought to be looking at them for evidences of God rather than for faults to criticize. They may not be as perfect (mature) as they ought to be, but look at the changes God has made already. See His power, His grace, His mercy and His patience. As we reflect on these things in our brother, it should help us to love God more as we are seeing Him evidenced in our loved one.

> *"Whosoever believeth that Jesus is the Christ is*
> *born of God: and every one that loveth Him that*
> *begat loveth him also that is begotten of Him. By*
> *this we know that we love the children of God,*
> *when   we   love   God,   and   keep   His*
> *commandments" (I John 5:1-2).*

How can we tell that we have real love for the brethren? We obey God.

If our local church dares to obey the Bible in church discipline, one of the accusations that we will face will be that we lack Christian love. However, true Christian love is obeying God and keeping His commandments. If I were to allow my children to grow up undisciplined, that is evidence, according to the book of Proverbs, (13:24) that I hate them and do not love them. If I love them I must chasten them betimes. Ponder verse 2 again:

> *"By this we know that we love the children of*
> *God,   when   we   love   God,   and   keep   His*
> *commandments."*

We don't act by whims or petulance; we treat others as God said they are to be treated. We must be obedient to God and His commandments in our relationship with our brothers and sisters, regardless of what it may cost us. Persecution may follow, but we must obey His commands, and they are not grievous.

CHAPTER 6

MARK # 6
LACK OF A CONDEMNING HEART AND ANSWERS TO PRAYER

"For if our heart condemn us, God is greater than our heart, and knoweth all things. Beloved, if our heart condemn us not, then have we confidence toward God" (I John 3:20-21).

If, in the light of the Word of God and the working of the Holy Spirit, our heart does not condemn us, then we can have a confidence toward God. However, it is possible that our heart will condemn us. That does not automatically mean we are lost. It also may mean that we are saved. Keep in mind that God is greater than our heart. We are not saved according to how we feel in our hearts.

People often say, "If I know my heart, I know I am saved." Well, our hearts may deceive us. Jeremiah 17:9 warns,

"The heart is deceitful above all things, and desperately wicked; who can know it?"

Our hearts may condemn us because of some unconfessed sin, or the devil has deceived us in some area and is accusing us falsely. If the latter is true, we may repent again and again, without getting any relief. It is impossible to get free of some sin of which we are not guilty. Thus, when our hearts condemn us we must examine as to whether the enemy of our soul has deceived us or whether you have an area of sin yet to be dealt with.

It is possible that our flesh natures may have gotten proud of how well we were living as a Christian and built up a few things beyond what God said to do. Then, when we failed in those our hearts begin to condemn us on things that are not really an issue with God. Not too many people have that problem today because few want to be stricter than God. Job's three friends were stricter with Job than God was, so that is a possibility. God said Job was perfect and upright in all his ways. God allowed the devil to try to find something wrong. The devil failed, but Job's three friends thought they could.

We need to be very careful that our wicked hearts not pull for looseness or pull for legalism, getting us away from Biblical standards. The devil is an extremist who cares little whether he gets us into the ditch on one side of the straight and narrow or on the other side. Hold to every Biblical standard, but be wary of what our own flesh and the devil may do to cause a condemning heart. The Bible promises that the pure in heart shall see God. If, in the light of God's Word, our hearts don't condemn us, what a blessing that is!

Notice that I John 3:22 begins with a conjunction;

> *"And whatsoever we ask, we receive of Him, because we keep His commandments, and do those things that are pleasing in His sight."*

(Some may want to treat answers to prayer as a separate mark of eternal life, but because of the conjunction I have kept the lack of a condemning heart and answers to prayer as one mark.)

I believe that prayer is the greatest privilege and ministry a saint can have. The apostles wanted to give themselves to prayer and the ministry of the Word, -- in that order, and with that priority. Jesus prayed before He preached. He lost sleep in order to pray before ministering. This is how important prayer is.

Chapter 6: Mark #6: Lack Of A Condemning Heart & Answers To Prayer

Prayer is the best way to take our spiritual temperature. How is your prayer life? The answer to that question will tell us how we are coming along in our Christian life. One of the old saints said, "What a man is on his knees, that he is and nothing more." When one has a constant flow of answers to prayer, his heart will be saying, "Hallelujah! Look what God is doing." Answered prayer and lack of a condemning heart are married together by that word "and".

I firmly believe that the Prayer Meeting is the most important meeting in the church. Occasionally someone will ask what we do at our Prayer Meeting and I just tell them we pray. Yes, we may sing a little and teach a bit, but our main purpose for gathering in the middle of the week is to pray. We pray because we expect God to answer. We believe that prayer is the birthright of every believer, and that it is vital for the heart to know that God hears and answers prayer.

Look at I John 3:22 again. The continual flow of answered prayer is a result of two things. First, we keep the definite commands of God. Our level of obedience will determine our level of prayer. If we decide that we will obey part way only, part way is all the further we will get in prayer. The more separated, holy and obedient we are, the more effective we will be in prayer.

The second reason that prayers are answered is that we do those things that are pleasing in His sight. That is love. First, we are commanded to obey. Second, we simply love. We ought to know God well enough that we can find things that He didn't command, but that would please Him.

Many years ago when my wife and I were dating, we were getting to know each other. We discussed our different backgrounds, what we thought marriage was and the husband/wife relationship. This was serious discussion with us. The matter of a wife being in submission to her husband and being obedient to him was settled. She asked what my favorite dessert was. No one had ever asked me that. I was just glad if there was dessert!

I responded, "pie". Then she wanted to know the kind of pie. That thought had never crossed my mind either, but I gave the answer, "Fruit pie". Not one to give up, she asked what kind of fruit was my favorite. I said, "Apple, peach, pear, plum . . . you know." She said, "Pear?" I wasn't about to confess that I had gotten carried away in naming fruit pies so I said, "Sure, pear pie".

She went home and asked her mother how to make pear pie. Her mother wondered about it, but understood when she was told that I liked pear pie. Believe me, my future wife made the best pear pie I had ever had. It was the first one I had ever had, and I enjoyed it. I had not commanded her to make a pear pie, but she so wanted to please me that she was willing to make it.

When we love someone, we are watching for that something extra we can do to really please. It is one thing to obey all commands, and quite another to make a special effort to please Him. We may be thinking, "God didn't tell me to do this; but I believe that if I do, a little smile may run across His face." I know God is a Spirit, but understand, I am speaking in a figurative way.

Do we know the kinds of things that may not be commanded in the Bible, but because of fellowshipping and spending time with Him, we believe those things would please Him? Following through on those will open up our prayer life and get the answers coming.

Before they were married my father went to visit my mother. He was a farm boy from Northwestern Pennsylvania, and she was a city girl from Hackensack, New Jersey which is just across the river from New York City. Obviously, there were many and great differences in their backgrounds. While they were visiting, she looked directly at him and asked, "Is there anything about me that you would like me to change?" He told her he didn't like lipstick, so she excused herself, went to remove it and never wore it again. Did she have convictions against it? No. Had he commanded the change? No, she wanted to please him. This kind of thing we do on a human level. What are we doing just to please God?

I John 5:14-15 states,

> *"And this is the confidence that we have in Him, that if we ask anything according to His will, He heareth us: And if we know that He hears us, whatsoever we ask, we know that we have the petitions that we desired of Him."*

Our hearts cease to condemn us. We obey and please God. Answers to prayer come repeatedly. We come to know God's will, and we ask and know that He is listening. When we know that He hears, we can expect the answer is coming, - that it will only be a matter of time. Do we have such confidence in our relationship with God that we can thank Him for an answer before it arrives? Can we make plans based upon knowing the answer that is coming? This is normal Christian living because this is eternal life.

A number of years ago I had a meeting to preach arranged in upstate New York. I felt impressed of God to make a trip out into Ohio, and make several stops along the way. I did not have enough money to pay for fuel and for food for my whole family. However, I had prayed and was convinced that if God did not send the money before we left, He would provide for us during the trip. We started out, traveled 400-500 miles, and made a few visits along the way. As we were getting into our van to leave a dear farmer friend, he reached into his wallet and said, "God impressed me to give this to you."

I thanked him, knowing we needed that gift to get to the next place. This was the pattern of the entire trip. We were able to buy our gas and feed our family. When we arrived safely at our home, we had one dollar left! I would have been foolish to go off on that trip if I had been living in disobedience to God.

We are living in such days of apostasy that it is hard to find genuine eternal life. Over the years I have tried to study the difference between death and life. At what point does a living person become dead? What is that thin line that we cross that determines death? We can give a Biblical definition – death is when the soul leaves the body. However, the soul leaving the body is a little difficult to analyze or measure. A better understanding of the difference between death and life would help us understand why we have appearances of life in a church, but, in actuality we may be looking at lost people who are still dead in trespasses and sins.

Some time ago I witnessed an unusual incident that may contribute understanding to this subject. At the outset, I want to state clearly that everyone involved in this was Bible-believing. There was no Charismatic leaning whatsoever.

A lady in her 80's whom I had known since boyhood, lay dying. She was in a hospital room where she had been in a coma. Her body functions were shutting down as she headed into "the valley of the shadow of death". My wife was with me as well as a former missionary with excellent Bible school training. This lady had known the dying woman nearly as long as I had.

There came a time when the breathing of the dying lady ceased, though the monitor on her heart continued occasionally letting out a little beep and showing a small jump in the line. At this point, she could not be declared "dead" though she no longer breathed; and for all practical purposes, her body had stopped functioning.

After quite some time the line ran flat on the heart monitor and stayed flat. The nurse noted this and said that certainly our friend appeared to have died but that a doctor would have to come and officially declare her dead. Several nurses had checked carefully; and there was no heartbeat, no breathing, and no blood moving through the veins. Perhaps half an hour after the line had gone flat, we were still waiting for a doctor to come.

The missionary lady turned to me saying, "Paul, I want to ask you to do a strange thing." I told her that if I could I would. She continued, "I want you to go over to her bedside and speak to her." Both the missionary lady and my wife followed me.

Let me interject here that I have spoken to dead people many times. About every time I preach, I am talking to some dead people, - spiritually dead folks, that is.

At the missionary's request, I spoke. The line on the monitor jumped, and there was a heartbeat. I don't know whether it jumped once or several times. The action was so strange and unexpected that I was hardly a passive observer.

We repeated this several times. On each occasion, the heart would pump. Evidence was clearly on the screen. No, I didn't raise her from the dead. However, if a doctor had been there, he would not have declared her "dead" while there was any response showing.

Do I understand why speaking to our friend's body elicited a sign that looked like life? No, but I fear that many folks in our churches show temporary signs of eternal life while under the preaching of the Word. God's Word is far greater than the word of any man. We accept temporary signs of eternal life as real eternal life. We have not distinguished the differences between real life and death.

If we are not careful and discerning, we will think people are saved – alive – when the mighty power of this Sword strikes down in their hearts; and there is a little "jump". I think this is what is described in II Peter chapter 2. The power of the Word of God cleans individuals up without their ever having been converted. The sow that was washed returns to her wallowing in the mire, and the dog returns to its vomit. We need to know what real eternal life is; or we will be deceived by the false "jump". Strong preaching can make some <u>look</u> right without <u>being</u> right.

It is important that we know the Scriptural marks of eternal life from the Scripture so that we can identify and separate that which is false from that which is real. It is particularly vital that we understand these marks when dealing with lost souls.

CHAPTER 7

MARK #7
INDWELLING OF THE HOLY SPIRIT

In I John chapter 3 and verse 24 we read,

"And he that keepeth His commandments dwelleth in Him, and He in him. And hereby we know that He abideth in us, by the Spirit which He hath given us."

The indwelling presence of the Holy Spirit is more than terminology and far more than a doctrinal statement. His presence should be a practical, personal realilty that is part of eternal life. God places the third member of the Trinity in our bodies which become His temple. Wherever we go, the Holy Ghost goes with us. He can be quenched and He can be grieved, for He is a person.

As far as I know, the before mentioned dying lady died lost. She knew Bible doctrine better than many fundamental preachers. She could quote Scripture better than most Bible school graduates. However, she never came to a conscious reality of doing business with the God of glory. She wasn't certain that there really was a God. She had a head full of knowledge but no experience in her heart. Many folks told her that she was probably saved and just didn't know it.

I believe that if we are genuinely born again we are going to know it. How can we walk around with the third member of the Trinity indwelling our body without His having any effect upon us? He is not a passive indweller. He is in there actively, and this is another way we can be certain we have eternal life.

He is there to bear witness with us that we are the sons of God. This is made plain in I John 5, verses 6 and 8. The Spirit is consciously working to bear witness that a person is saved.

Let me cite the example of a young man who had sought God for some time.

God had to deal with a number of areas in this young man's life, and God worked faithfully. He is now seemingly converted. His great concern had been a lack of the witness of the Spirit with his own spirit. He wasn't satisfied with head knowledge, doctrine, or explanation. He wanted the reality of eternal life. We are not talking about a subjective experience, but a definite experience of the Holy Spirit indwelling our bodies and taking control.

This Holy Spirit bears witness, but we are told in I John 4:1,

> *"Beloved, believe not every spirit, but try the spirits whether they are of God: because many false prophets are gone out into the world."*

When we have a spirit speaking within, don't assume that it is the Holy Spirit. There are many false spirits, and we are warned against believing just any spirit. In fact, we are commanded to try the spirits and find out whether we are hearing the Holy Spirit or a counterfeit. There are religious spirits that counterfeit the work of the Holy Spirit and deceive many souls. Some deceive until the point of death. Because the seduced ones never tried the spirits they go to hell thinking they were saved all the time. There are multitudes of people who believe that they are indwelt by the Spirit and have heard from the Spirit, but it is a counterfeit spirit.

I John 4:2-3,

> *"Hereby know ye the Spirit of God: Every spirit that confesseth that Jesus Christ is come in the flesh is of God: And every spirit that confesseth not that Jesus Christ is come in the flesh is not of*

*God; and this is the spirit of antichrist, whereof ye
have heard that it should come; and even now
already is it in the world."*

What is the ultimate checkpoint? Does the spirit confess
that Jesus Christ has come in the flesh? This is the measuring
stick and not whether the Spirit gives us good feelings or
whether He gives us peace. If the spirit does not confess that
Jesus Christ has come in the flesh, then it is the spirit of
antichrist. The Scriptures do not say that the spirit has to deny
that Jesus has come in the flesh. Just leaving that out is
revealing. Any spirit that is silent on the subject is not of God,
but is antichrist.

I can remember my dad cautioning me while I was yet a
boy, "Son, when you are dealing with error, don't watch so
much what they say; but watch what they neglect to say." Often
the place where truth is left out is where the error is lurking.

Some spirits deny that Jesus Christ is come in the flesh. That
is, they deny that He has always existed as God, and that He
came here sinless and lived here sinless by means of the
incarnation and through the process of the virgin birth. In
contrast, the Holy Spirit is going to bear witness of this Jesus
Christ and not of Himself. He will touch all those bases
mentioned and even more.

Not only will the Holy Spirit confess that Jesus Christ is
come in the flesh, but He will confess it repeatedly. Notice that
"confesseth" has the "eth" ending, which means ongoing. A
demon might mention that Jesus Christ is come in the flesh
once to try to fool us but the Holy Spirit will bring it up again
and again. Also, the Holy Spirit does not profess it, but He
confesses it. That means a touchstone of reality and experience
accompanies His confession. The Holy Spirit was part of the
incarnation, part of the virgin birth, and part of the earthly
ministry. The Holy Spirit will confess His death, burial,

resurrection, and ascension repeatedly to make it a reality in your souls. Anything less than this repeated confession means that the Holy Spirit is not dwelling within.

You, dear reader, may have many spiritual things said to you from within: but the source may be demonic spirits. That may sound too strong, but keep in mind that I saw the jump of a heartbeat in a corpse. Many people respond with a little jump once in a while without actually possessing eternal life.

> *"Ye are of God little children, and have overcome them: because greater is He that is in you, than he that is in the world" (I John 4:4).*

All those spirits that deny are silenced. They can profess but cannot confess that Jesus Christ is come in the flesh. We have overcome them. As Scripture states, greater is He is that is in you than he that is in the world. The Holy Spirit is far superior to all the demonic forces on the face of the earth. Satan and the demons do not let souls go that easily. They may cause us trouble, but we should have victory. This victory should be a way of life because everyone who has been saved has overcome Satan and the demons by the power of the Holy Spirit.

Look at I John 4:13:

> *"Hereby know we that we dwell in Him, and He in us, because He hath given us of His Spirit."*

God Himself dwells within us. We have God's Spirit and it is life-changing. II Peter 1 says that we become partakers of the divine nature. We have His Spirit and God's nature. That is a marvelous thing.

The indwelling of the Holy Spirit produces a multitude of ministries. He teaches us (I John 2:27). He bears witness (I John 5:6-8). He guides us. He convicts us. He seals us. He fills us. He anoints us (I John 2:27). He gifts us. He shows us. He empowers us. He enlightens us. He calls us. He sends us. He has already given birth to us. He prays through us on our behalf. He makes intercessions for us. He burdens us. He sanctifies us. He leads us. He fellowships with us. He produces faith, fruit, life, light and unction (I John 2:20). He gives us comfort and much more. Regarding the working of the Holy Spirit, we need to get back to the lines God drew.

Don't tell me that you cannot tell if the Holy Spirit is within you . He is busy!

Chapter 5 of 1 John

1Jo 5:1 *Whosoever believeth that Jesus is the Christ is born of God: and every one that loveth him that begat loveth him also that is begotten of him.*

***2** By this we know that we love the children of God, when we love God, and keep his commandments.*

***3** For this is the love of God, that we keep his commandments: and his commandments are not grievous.*

***4** For whatsoever is born of God overcometh the world: and this is the victory that overcometh the world, even our faith.*

***5** Who is he that overcometh the world, but he that believeth that Jesus is the Son of God?*

***6** This is he that came by water and blood, even Jesus Christ; not by water only, but by water and blood. And it is the Spirit that beareth witness, because the Spirit is truth.*

***7** For there are three that bear record in heaven, the Father, the Word, and the Holy Ghost: and these three are one.*

***8** And there are three that bear witness in earth, the spirit, and the water, and the blood: and these three agree in one.*

Continued on the next page:

9 If we receive the witness of men, the witness of God is greater: for this is the witness of God which he hath testified of his Son.

10 He that believeth on the Son of God hath the witness in himself: he that believeth not God hath made him a liar; because he believeth not the record that God gave of his Son.

11 And this is the record, that God hath given to us eternal life, and this life is in his Son.

12 He that hath the Son hath life; and he that hath not the Son of God hath not life.

13 These things have I written unto you that believe on the name of the Son of God; that ye may know that ye have eternal life, and that ye may believe on the name of the Son of God.

14 And this is the confidence that we have in him, that, if we ask any thing according to his will, he heareth us:

15 And if we know that he hear us, whatsoever we ask, we know that we have the petitions that we desired of him.

16 If any man see his brother sin a sin which is not unto death, he shall ask, and he shall give him life for them that sin not unto death. There is a sin unto death: I do not say that he shall pray for it.

17 All unrighteousness is sin: and there is a sin not unto death.

18 We know that whosoever is born of God sinneth not; but he that is begotten of God keepeth himself, and that wicked one toucheth him not.

19 And we know that we are of God, and the whole world lieth in wickedness.

20 And we know that the Son of God is come, and hath given us an understanding, that we may know him that is true, and we are in him that is true, even in his Son Jesus Christ. This is the true God, and eternal life.

21 Little children, keep yourselves from idols. Amen.

CHAPTER 8

MARK #8
CONFESS THAT JESUS IS THE SON OF GOD

"Whosoever shall confess that Jesus is the Son of God, God dwelleth in him and he in God" (I John 4:15).

The eighth mark of eternal life is this matter of confessing that Jesus Christ is the Son of God. There is, as previously mentioned, a big difference between confessing and professing. Confessing requires reality and not just words.

From time to time, there is a bomb blast in New York City. Within the hour, police stations are humming with calls from various groups claiming to have set off that blast. Only one, if any, actually did it, and the police try to sort out the confession from all the professions. Only one can make a true confession.

Today there are many people making professions of salvation to please Mom, or Dad, or the pastor or perhaps, the Sunday School teacher. A profession may make someone happy or get someone out from under pressure. That is not the mark that God gives.

There must be a vital reality to and evidence of the confession that Jesus is the Son of God. The life must evidence that Jesus is not just a man, but He is Almighty God. There must be evidence of God working through the life in a way that is beyond human ability. Almighty God's ability is related through a human vessel. When someone asks how something happened we confess that Jesus did it. We realize that His deity working through us becomes evidence to lost humanity. We become, in a sense, an extension of the incarnation because we confess that Jesus is the Son of God and that Almighty God dwells within. Our salvation ought to be evidence of our surrender to His Lordship and of those vows of salvation that we took. We talk about surrendering to His Lordship at the time of conversion, but it will show up on a regular basis in the life that follows. This can only be so because God gave us eternal life. Our human life and ability could never perform all of this. God's life is eternal by nature and was given to us so that we could live on a higher plane. We <u>must</u> live on this higher plane because we have eternal life. God has invested His life in us, and He expects us to live holy lives. In our lives He can clearly be seen in this world.

Some people profess that Jesus is the Son of God and has saved them, but their lives don't demonstrate that He helps them day to day. I learned of a young man in Israel who lived loosely and wildly, with dancing and flirting. One day he met the Lord up on Mount Carmel behind his home, and Jesus saved him.

He went home but didn't tell his mother. He just went about doing his regular duties. Within a week, his mother called him aside and said, "David, what is wrong with you? You don't react like my son. You've become a good boy. What has happened to you?" His reply to his mother was simple, "Jesus saved me, and I just wondered if you would be able to see it." It wasn't long before his mother was saved.

I wonder how many people would know us to be Christians if we never told them? We <u>are</u> to tell folks; but if we don't have a life that backs our testimony up, our words are rather hollow. We need to be able to confess Jesus.

Chapter 2 of I John deals with some that might talk eternal life but cannot walk it. Verses 22 and 23 say,

"Who is a liar but he that denieth that Jesus is the Christ? He is antichrist that denieth the Father and the Son. Whosoever denieth the Son, the same hath not the Father: but he that acknowledgeth the Son hath the Father also."

It is possible to deny Jesus with more than your mouth. You can deny him by your very life. Is your life backing up your words so that you are confessing Him, or is your life a denial of your words, making them an empty profession?

These are sobering thoughts but these are the marks that God has given us to help us know whether we are saved and have eternal life. For some it will bring rejoicing. We may go through a given situation and look back to say, "You know it is amazing! If I had thought about it I never would have expected that I would have behaved or reacted in that way. It must have been the Lord because that is not my nature."

Oftentimes we show what we are in the unguarded moment. Many can grit their teeth so to speak, knowing how and when to smile or say the right thing, behaving correctly when they know ahead that they are going to be in a spot. However, when a difficulty blindsides them it is a different matter. What is inside will come out at a time like that. God allows this to show what the true nature of the well is way down inside – sweet or bitter.

CHAPTER 9

MARK #9
VICTORY OVER THE WORLD

I John 5:4-5 says,

> *"For whatsoever is born of God overcometh the world: and this is the victory that overcometh the world, even our faith. Who is he that overcometh the world, but he that believeth that Jesus is the Son of God?"*

The ninth mark of eternal life is overcoming the world. Those who cannot overcome the world are lost. They have not been born of God. When one is born of God he can and will overcome the world. We may not have these marks showing one hundred percent in our lives, but we have a desire in our heart to please God. We are making progress, and we have a broken heart every time we fall short.

If we look carefully at these verses, we will note that the word is "overcometh". This does not mean that many years ago we had a victory. It means that we have been having victory, we are having victory; and because we have eternal life, by the grace of God, we will keep on having victory. We might stumble but God will keep us from falling.

Think on this simple illustration: a boat can be in the water, but it is dangerous when the water gets in the boat. Can you imagine someone carving a boat out of a big chunk of ice and pushing it out into a lake so they can fish for a while? The boat is of the lake. Some "professors" are of the world, and it won't be long before they will be <u>fully</u> worldly. It is important to keep the world out of your life.

I visited a missionary ministering down in the interior of Brazil. Our plan was to cross a river during rainy season. The river was a mile or two wide, though it looked more like twenty miles wide to me. We were in an aluminum motor boat, and the river was strewn with logs that had been washed downstream. We watched those logs carefully because you can imagine what damage they could do if they hit our boat broadside. We also had to consider the whirlpools caused by the flooding.

There were four of us in the boat originally designed for three, and we had a couple of oars in case the motor gave out. As we started out, I discovered that the boat had a small leak. While the others watched for the logs floating freely downstream, I grabbed a can and started bailing. I was not interested in discovering how much water we could take into the boat and still stay afloat. As far as I was concerned, the less water in the boat the happier I was.

As a Christian, that is how we ought to feel about the world. We ought to be overcoming the world and dumping it out. I fail to understand a Christian who is interested in how much of the world they can take in and still stay afloat.

Not only ought we to be in constant opposition to the world, but we are to have constant victory over the world. What is the world? It is the way of life, the way of thought, the set of styles, the set of attitudes, and the set of goals and motives by which this system around us operates. Satan is the god of this world system, and he leads it and controls it. He uses the world to keep his people conformed and controlled within his system. Christians need to be in absolute opposition to the world.

Look at chapter 2 verse 15:

> *"Love not the world, neither the things that are in the world. If any man love the world, the love of the Father is not in him."*

This would include Demas who left Paul, having loved this present world. "For all that is in the world, the lust of the flesh, and the lust of the eyes, and the pride of life, is not of the Father, but is of the world. And the world passeth away, and the lust thereof: but he that doeth the will of God abideth forever" (I John 2:16,17). This world is going to pass away. It is constantly shifting and changing. Yet people are caught and trapped therein.

> "Behold what manner of love the Father hath bestowed upon us, that we should be called the sons of God: therefore the world knoweth us not, because it knew Him not" (I John 3:1).

Anytime the world, led and controlled by Satan, understands us, there is something wrong in our lives. Anytime a church makes sense to the world, it may no longer be a real church. The world does not understand God's people because it did not understand Jesus. We ought to be a source of confusion and amazement to the world. We ought to live on such a level and by such means, motives, and goals that the world just cannot figure us out. Such is normal eternal life showing up in the Christian's life.

Look at verse 13 of chapter 3:

> "Marvel not, my brethren, if the world hate you."

Ponder that while looking back at verses 11 and 12:

> "This is the message that ye heard from the beginning, that we should love one another. Not as Cain, who was of that wicked one, and slew his brother. And wherefore slew he him? Because his own works were evil and his brother's righteous."

Cain's hatred of Able stemmed from the fact that Cain's own deeds were evil and he was of the world. Abel's were

67

righteous. Our righteous deeds are reason enough for the world to hate us. There ought to be ongoing evidence that the world does not understand us, like us, or agree with us.

I John 4:4-6 states,

> *"Ye are of God, little children, and have overcome them: because greater is He that is in you, than he that is in the world. They are of the world, and the world heareth them. We are of God: he that knoweth God heareth us; he that is not of God heareth not us. Hereby know we the spirit of truth, and the spirit of error."*

Brethren, the spirit of error is not revealed by whether somebody agrees with our doctrine. Rather, the spirit of error is revealed by our audience. If the world tunes in then it is the spirit of error at work. If God's people tune in, it is the Spirit of truth.

You can readily tell that a man is in error when he has the ear of the world. Any preacher, pastor, or evangelist who is acceptable and listened to by the world is not of God. If you want your church to be popular, it will not be right and holy, and you may not be saved.

The enemies of our Lord killed Him and they would like to do the same to all of His true followers of today. We have to overcome their attacks, their lies, and their persecution. We must do that by faith. We must live and overcome their system; for their system will destroy any church. It has done just that numerous times over the past number of years. Simply put, the world is no friend to God's people.

> *"And we know that we are of God, and the whole world lieth in wickedness"* (I John 5:19).

One of the unmistakable marks of eternal life is victory over the world. We must be separated from the world. The world lies in wickedness while we keep His commandments and do righteously. There is a gulf between us; and when the world tries to overtake us, we can enjoy victory. God has given us His own life that we might have the strength and ability to overcome the world. There is no excuse for a Christian to be worldly. We should despise the world because of its nature, location, god, motives, message, and desires. We must stand in total opposition to the world, for that is eternal life.

CHAPTER 10

MARK #10
A WITNESS IN OURSELVES

The tenth mark of eternal life is found in I John 5:10:

"He that believeth on the Son of God hath the witness in himself: he that believeth not God hath made Him a liar; because he believeth not the record that God gave of His Son."

The mark of believing is that there is a witness within. God doesn't leave us to our faulty memory, as we try to conjure up what the emotions of that moment may have been. God places within us a testimony and witness that will speak repeatedly, so that we can know we are saved. This is part of eternal life.

The Bible spells out for us the nature and operation of the witness that God puts within the believer. If we are truly His, we will have His testimony so that we won't need the testimony of men. His witness is far greater than that of men.

If we have no witness within, we need to examine very carefully what has happened. If the witness has been there but is no longer, consider what kind of sin has come in. That sin must be dealt with in order to hear the witness coming through clearly again.

The Bible spells out for us the nature and operation of the witness that God puts within the believer. If we are truly His, we will have His testimony so that we won't need the testimony of men. His witness is far greater than that of men.

Look at verse 7 of chapter 5:

"For there are three that bear record in heaven, the Father, the Word, and the Holy Ghost: these three are one."

This verse is hated by the devil, and he has removed it from as many Bibles as he could. This is the greatest verse on the Trinity that I know. It is not just the Trinity exists, but that the Trinity is active and cooperative. The three of the Trinity are one, and yet they are three together that bear record in heaven.

God the Father says, "This is one that I have saved. He repented towards Me, and I saved him." The Word, the Lord Jesus, continues, "My blood cleansed him and he is co-heir with Me. He is going to rule and reign with Me." The Holy Spirit adds, "I am the One who convicted him and drew him to the Savior. I birthed him into the family. He is truly saved." This united witness is in heaven. You cannot argue with such a witness.

It is wonderful to know that witness is in heaven and that one day we are going to be there. However, I like a witness now. The promise is that God put a witness in us. Verse 8 says,

"And there are three that bear witness in earth..."

It didn't say "on" earth, but rather, "in" earth. This is a witness that God put within our frame of dust. We have this treasure in earthen vessels that the excellency might not be of us but of God.

What exactly is this witness? It is the witness God speaks of in verse 10. He says there are three of them: the Spirit, the water, and the blood. These three agree in one. Just as the Trinity is agreeing up in glory, God has put a three-fold witness in us and it will be in agreement with what God has done in us. All three will testify without contradiction.

The first witness is that of the Holy Spirit. He is in us to tell us that He is there and has sealed us until the day of redemption. By Him we are born into the family of God, and He bears witness with our spirit. Even if He were the only witness we would have a lot. However, we also have the water speaking. What is the water? Ephesians 5 speaks of the washing of the water of the Word. The Word gets to speak. Jesus said you are clean through the Word which He has given unto you (John 15). The Word begins by saying, "I cleaned up your life."

The Bible is not just a book of doctrine and teachings. It is far more. It is a means to cleansing. When we are out in the world on a daily basis and the filth of the world bombards our ears and eyes, we may come home feeling dirty. Then we can sit down and read the Word. We may not remember a thing we read but it will cleanse us.

This story told by an African pastor illustrates this truth. He saw a lady returning from the village well. She had gone with her basket to carry water but her basket leaked. By the time she returned home, almost all of the water had run out. He questioned, "Sister, what good is it for you to go to the well with your basket; and when you return you have little, if any, water?" She readily replied, "Oh yes, but my basket is clean!"

There are times that we come to the Word to learn something, and there are other times we are just thankful that it has made us clean. I know people who read a little before they go to work to get fortified; and when they return home they take time to read more to get cleansed. Does the Word bear testimony that it has cleansed us, or is it just a textbook of doctrine, facts, and religion? Jesus said,

> "Sanctify them through Thy truth: Thy Word is truth" (John 17:17).

Does the Word sanctify us?

Let me illustrate. Suppose I began to read from a booklet, "This preacher has been expounding the Word for 54 years. He preached in tents, evangelistic meetings, and Bible conferences. He pastored in Georgia, North Carolina, and South Carolina. For many years, he taught in the morning camp meetings at Faith

Baptist Church in Gainesville, Georgia. Brother Ray Brown might respond, "That is me! That is me!" I didn't mention his name, but one might realize the description sounds like Brother Ray Brown.

When I read in the Bible, *"Wives, submit yourselves to your own husbands,"* some lady may respond, "That is me! It is no option. It has been my practice!" Or I may read, "Train up a child in the way he should go and when he is old he will not depart from it." Another may see herself in this truth, "That is me! That is what I have been doing and that is how it has been turning out!" Both ladies begin to see that the Word is bearing testimony. "Let no man despise thy youth but be thou an example of the believer . . .". Young people may say, "That is us!" It is the Word bearing testimony in their souls. Other young people look at that verse and say, "What a strange idea. Is that what I am supposed to do?"

When you read God's Word do you say, "That is what happened to me" or "that describes me!"? This is the witness of the Word within. In fact, one day you may come across something you didn't know was in God's Word but that you have already experienced. Others may regard the same truth coldly, saying, "Now, I wonder where this fits in my doctrinal structure?" That is not a witness. That is academics. We need to get back to hearing the witness of the Water of the Word down in our souls.

There is a third witness that says, "I want to speak up! I am the blood of the Lamb. Look what I did! I cleansed you from your sins, and by me you overcame Satan. By me you have boldness to enter before the throne of God." The Holy Spirit, the Word, and the Blood are speaking and they are all saying the same thing. You can say, "I have a witness within. People can think what they want to think and say what they want to say, but I have the witness in me! It is a three-fold witness and I know it is so." Eternal life makes the difference.

There are those who would say, "Well, let me see. Let me get my Bible. I wrote it down there. Back on October 17, 1993 in the evening service, I prayed to receive Jesus; so I know I must be saved. They wrote it in my Bible." There are no marks of eternal life in that.

We have a witness!

> *"If we receive the witness of men, the witness of God is greater: for this is the witness of God which He hath testified of His Son" (I John 5:9).*

Better than anything man would say is the witness of God, stirring down in the soul. God did not leave us in doubt as to whether or not we are saved. He wanted us to know!

CHAPTER 11

MARK #11
POSSESS JESUS

Moving on to the eleventh mark, look at chapter 5 verse 12:

"He that hath the Son hath life; and he that hath not the Son of God, hath not life."

Let me state the Reno Amplified Version of that: he that hath the Son hath life; and he that hath not the Son of God, - it doesn't make any difference what else he may have, - hath not life. Regardless of what our doctrine is or what we claim our experience is, or what our religious background is, if we don't have the Son of God, we are lost. We either have Jesus or we don't. If we don't have Jesus we are lost. It is very simple. We may have all the trappings, knowledge, experience, and recognition of man we want, but if we don't have Jesus, we don't have anything when it comes to eternal life. It is the possession of Jesus that makes all the difference.

Some of you may remember back in the early 1970's when Campus Crusade, with their distorted view of the gospel, came out with the "I Found It!" campaign. However, the Bible speaks of Him, and not of an "it." Churches are offering a gift. They are offering salvation, but they are bypassing Him, the Lord Jesus Christ.

I have heard many say, "Well, I received salvation." Where, in the Bible, are we told to receive salvation?

The Bible does say, *". . . as many as received HIM . . .".* We used to say, "Jesus saves!" Now they say that a decision, or prayer, or religion saves. Still, it is only Jesus who saves. Eternal life comes from the Lord Jesus Christ. He is a person and becomes our spiritual Husband. Do you have Him, dear reader, or have you settled for something less? All these marks become evidences of whether Jesus is present or not.

CHAPTER 12

MARK #12
LACK OF CONTINUAL SINNING

The twelfth mark is dealt with at some length in I John. Chapter 5 verse 18 explains,

> *"We know that whosoever is born of God sinneth not; but he that is begotten of God keepeth himself, and that wicked one toucheth him not."*

As we have already seen, the "eth" on the end of a verb lets you know that the action was not a one-time action. It was something that happens again, and again, and again, and is continuing to happen. The twelfth mark affirms that there is a lack of continual sinning.

Remember that the second mark was that we acknowledge that we are sinners. However, this mark states that we don't keep on sinning and sinning. We may stumble but we don't wallow in sin. The verse says that we know. There is no question about this; it cannot be debated or argued. Those who have been born of God do not and cannot live on in their sin. God will not allow it. He that is begotten of God is constantly working to keep himself out of sin. He is resisting sin, doing that which is righteous, and obeying the commandments of the Lord Jesus Christ.

The Scripture continues,

> *". . . that wicked one toucheth him not."*

That touch means that the Devil cannot put a hand of affection on our shoulder. He cannot place a hand of ownership on our back because he no longer owns us. He cannot put the touch on us to do his will. He might, from time to time, attack in the battle; but he cannot put that touch on us. We can and will have victory over Satan. We will work at keeping ourselves from sin and will not be satisfied to hang onto a besetting sin. God cleanseth us from ALL iniquity.

Chapter 3 verse 4 reads,

> *"Whosoever committeth sin transgresseth also the law for sin is the transgression of the law."*

We live among a generation that doesn't know what "sin" is. However, we know that sin is the transgression of the law. If we break the law, we have sinned. After we are saved we will not continuously transgress the law. We will look at the law. It states, *"Thou shalt have no other gods before me."* We will respond," I don't want any other; I only want Him as my God."

God's Word tells us that there are not to be any graven images. We realize that we wouldn't want anything to substitute for or try to remind us of God. He has done such a work in our soul that we don't need a reminder. In the company of my wife, it would be foolish to carefully scan a photo of her to try to refresh my memory as to what she looks like! If God indwells us and we are daily in fellowship with Him, we won't need any graven images to remind us of Him.

Since the law says,

> *"Thou shalt not take the name of the Lord thy God in vain,"*

it will make us angry when people drag His name through the mud. We will love Him and His name.

The law tells us to rest on the seventh day to keep the Sabbath. We will be thankful that there is a day set aside every week to worship God and rest.

When we find out the law tells us to honor our father and mother we will say, "Hallelujah!" One day we might be parents, and we would want to be honored. One of the marks of a converted child is that his attitude toward his parents changes. Saved children won't be disobedient to parents like they used to be. They won't be perfect, but there will be a definite change.

Since the Scripture commands, *"Thou shalt not kill,"* we will feel that we wouldn't want to murder anyone. We would rather try to reach them for Jesus.

Since the law says, *"Thou shalt not commit adultery,"* we may say, "The very thought is abhorrent to me. I don't even want the thought to linger in my mind."

The law goes on to say, *"Thou shalt not steal."* We may avow, "If it doesn't belong to me, and I didn't earn it, then I certainly won't take it."

To the command, *"Thou shalt not bear false witness,"* we will readily agree. "Everything about God has to do with truth. Why would I want anything else?" we concur.

And when we read, *"Thou shalt not covet,"* our hearts respond that we are totally satisfied with Jesus. we will know that God will give us anything we really need; and with that we should be satisfied. If He didn't give it to us or make it possible for us to get it, then He must not have intended for us to have it.

We will look at the law differently. Instead of it being ten rigid rules that we struggle to keep, we will say, "That is for me! He has done something in me, and my heart agrees with all of that."

Remember that sin is more than the transgression of the law. The Bible gives a second definition:

> *"To him that knoweth to do good and doeth it not, to him it is sin."*

If we have eternal life we keep this and will not only avoid doing the "Thou shalt nots"; but we will start doing the "Thou shalts." We will look for opportunities to do well and to do right.

A third definition of sin is, *"Whatsoever is not of faith is sin"*. We may say, "I have eternal life and I am not going to live in sin. I <u>will</u> live by faith. The Bible says that the just shall live by faith. I will find areas of my life where I can live by faith."

Occasionally I ask someone to preach; and he responds, "Well I would, but I don't believe I am capable." I may answer, "Wonderful! If you did feel capable I would withdraw the offer." I don't want someone preaching who thinks he can do the job. I want someone who feels he cannot, but that through God, he can.

If we are performing at the level spiritually of which we are capable, then we are in sin. God never intended for us to be able to handle the tasks He gives us. He expects us to function above what we are able, so that we will have to trust Him. That way, He alone will get the glory.

Look at I John 3:5:

> *"And ye know that He was manifested to take away our sins; and in Him is no sin."*

Jesus didn't come to save us in our sins; He came to take our sins away. If we don't want to be rid of our sins, then we can't have Him.

We have a generation of folks who want to hang onto their sins with one arm and lay hold of Jesus with the other. That is impossible. Those who have eternal life are not going to live with their sins; they have a Savior who took their sins away.

Verse 6 continues,

> *"Whosoever abideth in Him sinneth not: whosoever sinneth hath not seen Him neither known Him."*

If we belong to Jesus we will not keep on sinning. The antithesis is then, of course, true. If we continue sinning then we have never known Jesus and have not been saved.

Chapter 12: Mark #12: Lack Of Continual Sinning

See verses 7 and 8:

> *"Little children, let no man deceive you: he that doeth righteousness is righteous even as He is righteous. He that committeth sin is of the Devil for the Devil sinneth from the beginning. For this purpose the Son of God was manifested, that He might destroy the works of the Devil."*

Jesus saves us from our sins, and He destroys Satan's works in and through us. We are part of His plan of defeating Satan's program here on earth and bringing about God's program. We ought to be constantly on the offensive against any works of the Devil, any sin in our lives and any sin around us.

One might ask, "Are you going to clean up the whole world?" No, I cannot even haul away all the garbage in our county. However, that is no excuse to leave it on my kitchen floor! I can clean up my house, and my yard and may even pick up some garbage out in the street. We do what we can. If we who are really saved were on the offensive against sin, don't you think that might slow it down a bit? All too many have gone soft on sin. They won't stand against it. Jesus is manifest in our lives to destroy the works of the Devil.

> *"Whosoever is born of God doth not commit sin:*
> *for His seed remaineth in him: and he cannot sin,*
> *because he is born of God" (I John 3:9).*

You could ask, what happens if a Christian gets into sin and refuses to get out of it? Chapter 5 explains that there is a sin unto death. I don't say that you should pray for that Christian. Peter did not ask Ananias and Sapphira to repent and get cleansed. He just announced that they were headed for the cemetery. When a Christian gets far enough into sin, before God allows them to make a pattern of practicing sin, He will kill them. God does not play games.

Our whole nation is accustomed to game playing and amusements. God is not into that sort of thing. He is dead serious on the matter of sin. If we are really His, we cannot do that because He won't have it.

I have known people to start down that pathway. I have gone to the home and been willing to discuss their sin. Eventually I may ask them if they have bought their cemetery lots. I urge them to save their family the agony of deciding where to bury them. I encourage such a person to pick the spot out for himself since he seems in such a hurry to get there. I may start reading in I John 5, follow with Romans 8, and then proceed to Acts 5. I try to stay with them until they realize that God is not going to play games over their sin, but He will deal with it as He has warned.

If I give such a person hope that they may not need a cemetery lot yet, I may go on to read Hebrews 12. Usually they don't like the alternative to God's chastening. However, a person who is determined to continue in his sin makes it clear that he has never been born again. He is illegitimate. I may finish with, "I am going to sit back as your Pastor; and if you don't repent, we will soon find out whether or not you are saved." At that point, some are eager to get out of their sin.

We must understand that God is so holy He refuses to allow His children to go on and on in sin. When they are born into His family, it is literally impossible for them to continue in sin. They may physically do it, but God will not allow them to continue.

My own children might have been capable of some things, but actually they were incapable. I was their father and my wife was their mother and we would not tolerate certain behaviors. What other kids in the church might do, ours could not. Humanly, of course, they had the potential; but family-wise they could not. God, in essence, says, "You might have a flesh nature, and you may be able to get started on that. However, you are in My family. Thus, you cannot do that. I won't allow it."

When God won't allow it, that is a CANNOT just as clear as can be. If I could enforce not allowing certain behaviors in my family, you had better believe that the God of glory can enforce it on all of His children.

Look at I John 3:10: *"In this,"* ("this" being whether or not they can go on in sin), *"the children of God are manifest, and the children of the Devil."* This is clear. What we can and cannot do will indicate whether we are children of God or children of the Devil.

A pastor friend whose church had grown cold spiritually was frustrated over their refusing to respond to preaching and praying. On a Sunday evening, in disgust and great disappointment, he left them with these words, "You refuse to respond to my preaching, my counsel, my pleas, or my prayers. I want you all to find a bar and see if you can get drunk. It is very probable that some of you can get away with it. If you find that you just can't do that, then maybe you will realize that God has put a limit on how far you can go. Perhaps that will help you to repent and amount to something for God!"

I am not recommending this pastor friend's approach. However, if you want to find out if you are saved, push the sin issue; and you will find out. The Devil's crowd can push the limits and get by. They can, indeed, make a profession, but God says they are showing to whom they really belong. They never have been saved and received eternal life.

> *"Whosoever doeth not righteousness is not born of God, neither he that loveth not his brother"* (I John 3:10b).

This simply repeats what we saw earlier. The marks of eternal life all fit together like a puzzle. They are interwoven. I have tried to separate them a bit so that we can see if we really have eternal life. If we do, there is something in our soul saying, "That is me! Hallelujah! That is me!"

Others of us may be thinking, "What is all this about? Is this eternal life? Does that much really happen?" Let these marks of eternal life help us to examine where our souls. Those who merely think they are saved might find out what it would be like to be truly saved. God may make them thirst and hunger after righteousness. They may seek after the Lord and repent of their rebellious ways.

Look to Jesus, dear reader. See if you can trust Him to wash you from your sins and put you into His family. He alone can make you a new creature and show you clearly what the true child of God possesses.

INDEX OF WORDS AND PHRASES

ABOUT THE AUTHOR

J. PAUL RENO has been a pastor in Ohio and Maryland since 1968. During this time he has also been involved in church planting, training men for the ministry and speaking on mission fields in Europe, the Middle East, Africa, South America and Mexico. The church he presently pastors has sent millions of dollars to missions. He continues to speak at various Bible conferences, camp meetings and local churches. He presently serves on the Board of Directors for the Conversion Center, which is headquartered in Hagerstown, Maryland. Pastor Reno recently was honored with the prestigious award, "Defender of the Scriptures," by the King James Bible Research Council.

He is also the author of *To Fight or Not to Fight, Daniel Nash: Prevailing Prince of Prayer, Investing for Eternity, Studies in Bible Doctrine* as well as over fifty pamphlets and booklets on salvation, the Christian life, Bible doctrine and the King James Version. His wife, Carolyn authored *Almost But Lost*, available as a free ebook download at:

http://www.theoldpathspublications.com/Pages/Free.htm.

www.ingramcontent.com/pod-product-compliance
Lightning Source LLC
Chambersburg PA
CBHW062019040426
42447CB00010B/2071